Kid Capitalist

What Every Kid Should Know About Owning a Business

By Tobe Brockner

Kid Capitalist
by Tobe Brockner
© 2014 by Tobe Brockner

To purchase copies of *Kid Capitalist* in large quantities at wholesale prices, please contact Aloha Publishing at alohapublishing@gmail.com.

Cover Design: Marshall Nichols, www.vsquaredcreative.com
Illustrator: Rani Child
Interior Design: Fusion Creative Works, www.fusioncw.com
Primary Editor: Amy Larson

Print ISBN: 978-1-61206-090-3
eBook ISBN: 978-1-61206-092-7
Library of Congress Control Number: 2014936530

Published by Aloha Publishing
Printed in the United States of America

To my own two little capitalists,
Beau and Scarlett.
I love you more than you'll ever know.

Doing well is the result of doing good.

That's what capitalism is all about.

– Ralph Waldo Emerson

Contents

A Note to Parents

A few years ago, I asked my then seven-year-old son, Beau, what he wanted to be when he grew up. He gave me the standard seven-year-old boy answers: policeman, fireman, astronaut, super hero.

Since I'm a business owner, I asked, "Well, what about owning your own company?"

"What?" he said, "I didn't even know you could do that!"

"Well, what do you think *I* do, knucklehead?" I joked.

Beau replied, "I don't know what you do."

It dawned on me then that Beau's not knowing what I did was my fault. Clearly I'd been derelict in my responsibilities as both a father and an entrepreneur, and this was a travesty, since I feel being an entrepreneur is one of the noblest of callings.

From that point on, I brought Beau and his younger sister, Scarlett, to work with me on certain days. I showed them what I did and got them involved in my business. They were fascinated by the notion that I could create money from an idea. They didn't think in those terms before I introduced the concept of entrepreneurship to them. They knew that people went to work, but how money was made was sort of fuzzy. I wanted to show them specific ways to make money. I told them, "This is what I do. These are the services my company provides, and people pay us money to do it."

They were completely enthralled, utterly captivated by this new world.

I wanted my children to know that the option of starting, building, and running a company was well within their reach.

Options. That, in essence, is what this book is all about: showing our children that they, too, can be entrepreneurs, not simply another employee in the corporate world. This is an attempt to present another choice for making their way in life.

Of course, being an entrepreneur isn't for everyone. My children and your children may not want to own their own business, but they should always know that it is an option.

After that first conversation with Beau, I began having regular business discussions with him and his sister. I explained the concept of trading value for value. I talked about what it meant to be a leader. I told them stories about my clients, about ideas that had failed, and about the success I had experienced. I educated them on the concept that a person could have an idea, extract it, package it, price it, and sell it to the marketplace.

Beau has begun to be a very active entrepreneur. He's discovered that there are services he can offer that people will actually pay for. He's started a business raking leaves, since there are people who don't want to rake. He's traded and sold football cards, shoveled snow, and created and sold friendship bracelets. He's beginning to think in terms of, "What can I do that most people don't want to do or don't have time to do, that they'd be happy to pay me for?" It's been a huge mental shift for him.

Over the years, main themes emerged from the discussions I had with the kids. I began to write them down in a journal, along with why I believed those themes were important, along with other things that I especially wanted my two kids to know. You are holding the result of that journaling in your hands.

What Your Child Can Expect From This Book

I tried to simplify the complexities of what I've learned as much as possible. This book isn't meant to be just another how-to manual for starting a business; it's more about what I think is important when running a business and about being a decent human being. The lessons are told in a business context, but they're really life lessons as well.

I hope that presenting the information in a simple, easy-to-read format will pique your child's curiosity and set him or her on a path of newfound discovery, one of exciting possibilities.

Your child will learn why businesses are crucial to our economy, how to be a great leader, how to understand and create value, how to treat employees, how to live a balanced life, how to follow his or her passion, and many other topics. This isn't a comprehensive treatise on the subject, but I truly believe this will better prepare children to live the life of an entrepreneur and to become a more valuable citizen of society.

What You Can Do

Each year I host an event called The Young Entrepreneur's Workshop. This free two-day event is designed to teach kids the ins and outs of starting and running their very own businesses.

During the second day, we divide the group into teams and give them a half dozen random items, along with a roll of duct tape. The goal is to create a product using only the items they have at their disposal. They then have to name it, price it, put a marketing plan together for it, and present it to the rest of the group. It is extremely entertaining to see the wild and crazy ideas these kids come up with, which is exactly the point.

We do not inhibit these children in the least. We encourage them to let their imaginations run wild, to think about solving problems in unique and wacky ways, and to simply *think* with no restraint. To *imagine*. To *create*.

This is what today's children need. They have enough people in their lives telling them to be practical, to stop dreaming, and to take the less risky path. We need our kids to feel safe expressing "crazy" or "unrealistic" ideas.

I'm certain Facebook founder Mark Zuckerburg's idea of creating a huge social platform that would be a connection point for a billion people was considered by many to be insane at one point in time.

But as Albert Einstein once said, "For an idea that does not first seem insane, there is no hope."

Over the past 100 years, some of our greatest inventions, innovations, and companies have come from a person or group who had a crazy idea. It is my hope that you will read this book along with your child. Encourage him or her to imagine the vast possibilities our era has to offer, and applaud the unrealistic, the crazy, and the different. Help your child realize that human potential is virtually unlimited, and that they can be the one to someday change the world.

Have fun,

Tobe Brockner

Introduction

You probably picked up this book or it was given to you because you have an interest in one day owning your own business. If that's the case then I applaud you; the world needs more entrepreneurs like you!

Owning a business will be one of the most challenging and rewarding experiences of your life. The beauty of being an entrepreneur is it's the one profession where you actually get paid to use your imagination. Imagine that! People will pay you to come up with and implement ideas! To me, there is no greater thrill than to see your ideas and hard work pay off this way.

Whether you want to own your business or not, I think you will find some useful information in the pages of this book. The twelve principles I outline here aren't just for being a better business owner. They're also for being a better employee, friend, sibling, and human being.

How to Use This Book

This isn't a "how-to" start your own business kind of book. There are lots of those kinds of books out there for you to read and I would encourage you to explore your local book store or library if you are interested in the mechanics of running a business.

This book is, however, more about the things I have learned over the last decade that have helped me in both business and in life. As you read through the chapters, think about how you can apply the principles you are learning to all aspects of your life, not just in business.

For example, in chapter 6 you will learn what it means to be a Servant Leader. Being a good leader isn't just important in your business, but will help you set a good example for your siblings or your friends. Use this new knowledge to help guide you to a better life.

Keep Me Posted

I hope that you enjoy reading Kid Capitalist as much as I enjoyed writing it. I would love to hear your thoughts about the book and business. Please feel free to send me an email with any questions or comments that you may have to tobe.brockner@gmail.com.

Good luck on your journey!

Tobe Brockner

Businesses are Good

At some point in your life, you will probably hear that businesses are only driven by money, and that business owners don't care about society or helping people. You will probably also hear that having government programs in place to "protect" people from business is the only option available to us. I am here to let you know that this isn't the case.

The truth is, businesses are not these big, evil, money-grabbing entities. Businesses are ways for ordinary people to lift themselves up, to make better lives for themselves. Businesses create jobs and eliminate poverty. As we move forward, there are going to be more and more attacks on business owners and entrepreneurs. At some point in your life, you'll be told that businesses do more harm than good, and that's just not true.

Doing More Good than Harm

I want you to know that businesses are good. Think about it: because of businesses, you don't have to grow your own crops. You don't have to build your own car, or your own house, or do any of the things we take for granted. Businesses do all of that for us, improving our lives by making things easier and more convenient.

Businesses also generate money and employment, creating opportunities for people through jobs. Businesses pay taxes that are used to build roads, bridges, and schools. Businesses benefit society as a whole; so the more successful the business, the more our society benefits.

Businesses might not have the ability to take care of everyone, but then again, when you look at the multiple ways businesses are helping groups of people as a whole, they really *do* take care of everyone because they provide for society in the ways listed above. We all benefit when businesses are healthy, growing, and making money.

Advantages of Owning a Business

If you're a business owner, one of the biggest advantages is that you're not relying on someone else to determine your value. You're rewarded based on your work and the value you bring. Employers pay employees a certain amount, based on how valuable they view that employee to be. It's generally just up to your boss whether you're doing a good job or not.

If I'm a business owner, the people who pay me are not my employers, but rather several different clients. As a group, these clients view me as valuable, and I determine my own value with them by what I charge. When I decide I'm only going to attract those clients or customers who believe the value is there, I set the value. I don't depend on any single person (like an employer) to do that for me. When most people are saying to themselves, "Why can't I move up in the company?" or "There's a pay ceiling, and I can only go so far," as a business owner, for me that's not true.

I can go as far and as high as I can climb, based on my efforts and my own sense of what I bring to the table. So can you.

That's a huge advantage.

Other advantages include:

- Setting your own hours
- Choosing who you want to work with
- Being your own boss
- Giving back to the community
- Building a valuable company that you can one day sell or pass on to your own kids

Not as Risky as You Think

Some people think that owning a business is risky because you won't have the "safety net" of an employer. I think we all need to redefine the idea of what is risky. Remember, if you go to work for an employer, there's one person you have to please. If that person doesn't like you, or if you don't do exactly as that person says, your job is in jeopardy. They can fire you.

If you own a business, you have a lot of different customers, not one boss. If a client decides they don't want to do business with you, that's okay. You've probably got fifteen or twenty more clients who do want to do business with you. Sure, you don't want to intentionally anger a client, but if one does happen to decide to stop doing business with you, you can get more clients to pick up the slack.

That's why I think owning your own business is the complete opposite of risk; it's actually way less risky.

Ways to Determine if You'd Make a Good Entrepreneur

Are you creative?

While that's not exclusive to entrepreneurs, it's a telling point. In order to be successful as an entrepreneur you must be able to solve problems effectively, and solving problems effectively requires the ability to see solutions to problems that others can't. This is creativity at its finest.

You will also need to come up with ways to differentiate yourself from your competition, or other companies in your industry. It could be that you offer better prices or higher quality goods. Maybe you have a great store location or offer free shipping. There are hundreds of ways to set yourself apart.

I think all people have creative genes within them, even if they don't think so. The key to becoming a great entrepreneur is to recognize that for what it is and be willing to say, "I'm creative. I'm a creative person, I think outside the box, and I can come up with different solutions to problems that most people wouldn't think about."

You've probably heard of Post-it® notes, right? Well, what you may not know is that Post-It® notes were created by accident. The scientist who invented them, Spencer Silver, was trying to invent a super-strong adhesive, but instead accidentally created a weaker adhesive that could be used over and over. Once he applied this to the back of a small piece of paper, the Post-it® note was born!

It would have been easier for Dr. Silver to simply discard the weaker adhesive, but he saw that there was a use for the product he had created, and that sparked a billion dollar business.

Do you have an ego that can handle doing things many people would consider menial or below them?

If you want to succeed as an entrepreneur, many times you need to accept that there's no job too low for you, and decide to do whatever you have to do. Think of the people who own a McDonald's franchise. The number of franchise owners who once started out as a cashier or fry cook is extremely high. There's a reason for that. They must have said to themselves at one point, "There's nothing in this company I can't do; there's no task within this company that I'm not willing to do." That might be an even more important distinction: that they're *willing* to do those things. There's also a difference between hard work and work ethic. Although it sounds like the same thing, there are people who work very hard that would still never dream of sweeping the floors or cleaning out the milkshake machine. Hard work and the willingness to do what others won't do are great determining factors for whether you'd make a good entrepreneur or not.

I say that this attitude is important because when you first start your business, there may not be anyone but you to do all the jobs that need to be done in a new company. You may not have any employees just yet and no one to help you. If you don't do it, then who will?

Are you motivated by the duty to serve others?

When people become doctors, most will make a promise called the Hippocratic Oath. The promise basically states: "First, do no harm." The very first thing they promise to do is heal others. There is a perception that people choose to become doctors because doctors make a lot of money. In reality, the main reason a person might want to become a doctor may have nothing to do with money. Most doctors want to help society by healing and curing people, and the money comes as a result of doing that. I think we can take that idea to the business world.

Entrepreneurs don't necessarily start businesses just to make money, although that might be an end goal. Entrepreneurs are often motivated by the duty to serve others and to help others solve their problems. The better they do that, the more people will want to do business with them, and the more money they'll make. For example, if a person builds websites for a living then it would serve her well to think constantly about the different ways she could take her designs to the next level. If her focus is continually on how she could better serve clients, then I can promise that the money will come, because people want to do business with those they feel care about them and will treat them right.

On that note, you should know that you can have the best of both worlds. You can serve a higher purpose and make a nice living for yourself; you don't have to pick one or the other. Much of the time, society tries to force us into the notion that we have to choose, and that doesn't sit well with me at all. You can have both. The doctor in our example above can focus on healing people and making money. The web designer can bring lots of value to her clients and they will pay her handsomely for it.

What it all really comes down to is this: How can you best help others solve their problems?

That's what it is about, no matter what you are selling or what you are offering. At the end of the day, you're really just trying to solve another person's problem. You will most likely succeed if you can look at your business through that lens first, the lens of, "I'm going to do the very best that I can to solve this problem in a unique and valuable way." Eventually people will pay you for your creativity and the money will come.

Purpose First, Profits Second

A lot of times, when someone has an idea for a new business, they filter the idea through this qualifier:

Will it make money?

That's the first thing they say, the first thing they think. If the answer is yes, they move forward. If it's no, they won't. I used to be that way, too. Some of my ideas never made a dime and were spectacular failures. Some ideas made a lot of money.

I found that if I focused only on money and profits, at the end of the day I felt empty, like something was missing.

My work had no meaning; it was just a means to an end, and that end was all about acquiring more wealth. I eventually asked myself, "Why am I running this race? What is it all for?"

That was a very empty way for me to live. When I began looking for opportunities to serve – to do some good within our society and make an impact – then I was happier, and the money naturally took care of itself. I began to make a difference in people's lives, whether it was in the community, with my employees, or with my vendors. I saw that what I was doing was directly impacting people's quality of life, and I began to attract people who felt the same way, people who wanted to help.

In my own business I do many things to give back to the community, one of which is a series of workshops for people who are struggling financially. One morning I had an interview on a local radio station to promote these workshops. After the interview my cell phone rang. It was a local business owner who said he had heard my interview and wanted to help. We became friends, and he has hired my company to help him with some of his marketing. By living my purpose I was able to attract this gentleman who appreciated my values and felt the same way I did.

Once I started living like that, looking more closely at how I could be of service to those around me as opposed to just making money, profits went up.

More than Money

I used to end each day with a couple of questions: "Did we make money today?" or "Did we hit our numbers and make a profit today?"

After I decided to begin living my purpose, I instead began asking myself at the end of each day, "Did we live our purpose today?"

I knew that if we lived our purpose and stayed true to our core values of being who we were and who we wanted to be, profits would naturally follow.

If you have too many days in a row where your answer to that question is "No," then something needs to change. Asking that question on a daily basis serves as a moral compass, and keeps you focused on the task at hand, which is to serve a higher purpose, not just chase profits.

Integrity Pays Off

Let me give you an example of this from my own life. In my business, one of our core values is integrity.

I once had someone sent to my company for a bid on a project. It was a project we could have done, but it wasn't necessarily our specialty. In addition, doing that project would have detracted from some of the other projects we were working on at that time, projects that did match our specialties. I felt that we weren't going to be able to give the customer the time or attention they needed in order to make their project work. So, I turned the project down, even though it meant giving up a sizable amount of money. I told the potential customer I didn't feel comfortable doing a bid, and that I didn't feel it was in their best interest to use us. I then referred them to an expert in that particular area. Walking away from the conversation, I felt better than I would have felt if I had bid the job.

I want to make sure that when people do business with me, they get exactly what I promised I'd give them, and in some cases over and above what they were promised.

A week later, the client I had referred sent another client my way who was a good fit, so we ended up making money anyway. Had I not done what I believed in, and lived the core value of integrity, we could have angered and alienated that potential client because we might not have done the job as well as we should have. That relationship would have burned up. Sure, we would have made the money, but it would have had a long-term negative impact on the business. By staying true to my integrity,

I built an even stronger foundation with that potential client, and established long-term trust in my company that I wouldn't have had otherwise.

Besides integrity, my company has several other values that we strive to live by. In fact, we have a created company chart that represents our values and how we plan to implement them for our Customers, Employees, Vendors, and Society as a whole. Down the left side we listed our values and across the top are the different groups we want to impact. This created a matrix, like the one below, and then we just filled in each box with action items to achieve that goal.

We Value:	Employees	Vendors	Clients	Society
Generosity				
Results				
Integrity				
Team-Work				
Self-Reliance				

As an example, under the Employee section for the value of Generosity we might write in that box, "We will pay our employees above-average wages, remember significant events in their lives, and reward them for living our company values."

For Clients under the value of Self-Reliance, we might write, "Help clients find areas where they can do things cheaper or faster than we can do them. Provide them with educational material that will help them with that."

Your values can be any that are important to you. There are no right or wrong answers here. As long as the values you choose are important and authentic to you, then you are on the right path. The key is to constantly be on the lookout for ways to live the values you have chosen. This is truly what living your purpose is all about.

Follow Your Passion

When I was about twelve years old, I wasn't the best student. For some reason, school didn't appeal to me, and I didn't make good grades. I didn't do well in such a structured environment, and as a result, one of my report cards wasn't so hot. My dad kind of came down on me pretty hard. He said, "What are you going to do if you don't make good grades in school? If you don't make good grades, you'll never get into a good college, and you'll never get a good job. What are you planning on doing with your life, if you don't make good grades?"

I remember telling him, "Oh, I'll just be a professional football player."

He said, "There's no way you'll be a professional football player. No way. You're not big enough, you're not fast enough, and you're not going to be athletic enough.

You're a good football player, but you're not going to be an NFL type. You just don't have the genetics for it."

Everything he said was completely true, but even so, I was completely crushed and devastated.

To my dad's defense, I was his first child and raising your first child can be challenging. I think it would have been much better for me had he then followed up with something like, "You have a certain skill range, and within that range, you can be anything you want to be. If you go outside that range, you're not going to do as well on either side of the spectrum. Your strongest point is not math, so being a math professor is probably not going to happen, and you probably wouldn't be happy anyway."

If you are good at, say, interacting with people and like to travel, you may be well suited to work in the travel industry or in international business. Your goal is to find out what you are good at and what you really enjoy doing within the range of skills that you have.

Pinpoint Your Passion

When I talk about passion, I guess what I'm really talking about is energy. It's following what gives you the most energy in your life. As Warren Buffett says, "What gets you to tap dance to work every day."

Passion is that which gives you the most energy. It's something you enjoy doing within the natural range of your own skill set.

Many people confuse blind passion with just doing what they love and thinking that the money will follow. That's false and misleading. I love sitting in a hammock and eating pizza, but haven't yet figured out a way to get someone to pay me to do that. I'm very passionate about those things, but that's not the sort of passion I'm talking about. I'm talking about what gives you *energy*. Working within your skill set gives you energy because those skills are things you're really, really good at *and* the things you enjoy doing.

There are also some things I'm really good at that I hate doing. Those aren't going to be long-term, viable solutions for me because if I do them, I'm going to be miserable. There are also things I love to do that I'm not very good at, and that's not going to work either, because no matter how passionate I am, I'll never make any money doing them.

For me personally, I am really good at consulting with clients, but it isn't my favorite activity to do. On the other hand, I love graphic design, but am horrible at creating things myself.

The key to your long-term happiness will be to find something that you're really good at and love doing.

Open Your Mind, Stay Curious

One of the mistakes people and parents make is not exposing children to as many different things as possible. A man who's a veterinarian has a high likelihood of having his children grow up to be veterinarians or working in the medical field, as opposed to other children with a non-veterinarian parent. Sometimes children live within a very narrow range, being exposed to very little, because what they are seeing almost every day pigeonholes them.

I think the world has probably missed out on having incredible physicists, engineers, and doctors who instead became attorneys or professors or whatever, because they weren't exposed to other possibilities as children.

When you were younger, say four or five years old, did grownups ever tell you to stop asking so many questions? I know that happened to me. But that's how children discover the range of things they're good at: by asking questions, by being curious about *everything*. In order to fully explore that range, natural curiosity should not be hampered. Adults should never let their kids' curiosity die out, and you should never stop being curious either.

As we get older, our curiosity might die down some, but we can maintain it by still looking around and seeing what the world has to offer. With the Internet available, there's no excuse for not exploring.

The only limitations we have lie within us. We need to preserve the same curious nature that little children who constantly ask questions have.

To me, a part of discovering passion is being exposed to and figuring out what you really love doing, and what you are naturally good at, within the genetic and natural skill set you've been blessed with.

A great example of someone who did this is Blake Mycoskie of TOMS Shoes. He didn't set out to be a shoemaker; he set out to make an impact on the world, one that benefited society. Blake created a program called One for One®, where every time someone buys a pair of shoes from TOMS, the company donates a pair of shoes to a child in need. Blake isn't passionate about shoes necessarily, but he is passionate about providing shoes for kids who need them. He could have done anything; it didn't have to be shoes. It could have been one-for-one hats or glasses. In fact, they have recently added eyeglasses to their One for One® program. For every pair of eyeglasses you purchase, TOMS will donate a pair to a child in need.

Steve Jobs, the founder of Apple, did the same thing: his whole purpose was to design beautifully simple and functional products. It didn't have to be computers; it didn't have to be Apple. He might have been just as happy going into the restaurant business, creating elegant, beautifully designed, palate-pleasing dishes on a grand scale for the largest restaurant chain in the world.

For these guys, it wasn't necessarily work that got them going; it was an understanding of what their skill sets were, and then finding something within those skills that they really, really enjoyed doing.

How to Tell When You're Not Working Within Your Passion

When you're not working within your passion, there are telltale signs:

- If you're feeling anxious.
- If you're not having fun anymore.
- If you dread getting up each day.
- If you dread going to work.
- If you're not energized anymore.
- If you're not feeling a charge from what you're doing.

If this is going on, chances are you're not doing what you're supposed to be doing.

Steve Jobs said this about passion: "If today were the last day of my life, would I want to do what I am about to do today? And whenever the answer has been 'no' too many days in a row, I know I need to change something."

It can be easy, though, to get caught up in the trap of, "Well, I'm not having fun, so this must not be my passion." Passion doesn't mean you have to be "on" all the time, or mean you'll always be happy. Get it out of your head right now that you'll always be doing the things you love, or what gets you amped up. That's just not always going to happen.

What you're looking out for is the realization that you're feeling discontent or anxious for too long. If that's the case, it's probably time to reassess. That doesn't necessarily mean you're in the wrong business; it could just mean you've gotten yourself into a rut. Maybe you have the wrong people around you, or you're not attracting the type of clientele you would like. You could be doing what you love all day, but if, for example, you have clients who are cheap, unrealistic, or demanding, you're not going to be having a very good time, even while doing something you love.

Working Within Your Passion is an Option

It's true that business owners have to work hard and do lots of things most "normal people" with typical careers wouldn't have to do, but being an entrepreneur gives you a level of freedom – a sense of being in control of your own destiny. I think that benefit is getting lost today in the way adults talk to kids about career opportunities and options for down the road.

When I was a kid, I never thought of owning my own business and wasn't told that was an option, even though my dad and grandfather owned businesses. I had this entrepreneurial blood running through my veins, but being my own boss was never really presented to me as an option. I didn't talk with my parents much about my future career. They'd ask, "What do you want to do when you grow up?" but didn't explain the choices available to me.

When I went to college I was trained to be a mid-level manager at a mid-sized company. I knew from the get-go that wasn't going to help me at all. That wasn't what I wanted to do. I wanted my own company.

I remember the day I made that decision. I was only eighteen, and it was the week before high school graduation. I was sitting in the back of a pickup truck with a friend, talking about what we'd do after we graduated. He asked if I'd go to work for my dad at his finance company.

I told him, "I don't know. I might."

My friend said, "What are you going to call it, Brockner and Son?"

I said, "No. We'll call it Brockner and Father."

Right then and there, I knew I wanted to own my own company, to be the boss – the one who hired employees, ran the whole operation, and motivated everyone. I had no idea how I was going to do it, but the *how* or *what* wasn't as important as the feeling I got when I thought about being an entrepreneur. Business A, B, or C, it didn't matter. I had just figured out for myself that being my own boss was a viable career option.

Do Something Else

When a cousin and I graduated from college, my grandfather-in-law, who was a pharmacist for a large grocery chain for many, many years, told us, "Look, you need to get a steady job at a company that has a good pension and retirement plan. You work for them for twenty-five, thirty, or forty years, and you'll be set."

That's what he did, but he lost his pension, and his company benefits got cut. He had been at their mercy. When he passed away a while later, he was completely broke. To me, that was tragic. Being a business owner seemed far less risky than being an employee at a mid- to large-sized company for thirty years. To me it was the definition of a grave, since a rut is really just a shallow grave. That was what he had been in, living a day-to-day existence that had no real meaning or purpose. Every single day, he had nothing to get excited about, and he had no control over the way things went; that was left up to someone else.

After our grandfather walked away, I looked at my cousin and said, "He's completely broke and he's giving us advice, telling us to do the exact same thing. I'm not doing that. I'm going to start my own business and control my own future. I'm not going to leave it up to simply working for a company and trying to rely on their pension."

The main difference between entrepreneurs and corporate manager-types is that managers live in micro worlds, the little bubbles of their departments. If they don't enjoy their day-to-day activities, they might feel they have nothing else to live for. The entrepreneur lives in a macro world, a much larger bubble. He lives in the future, extracting ideas to create a long-term, big-picture view of his business. That makes the day-to-day minutia of what entrepreneurs do much more bearable. Because we as entrepreneurs can see down the road, we'll put up with the less-than-enjoyable things of today, knowing those things are going to positively affect the future.

I'm not saying that being a corporate manager is bad, and I know some corporate managers who are very good at what they do and who are happy. But there's a whole other world of possibility out there.

So, Focus not on passion, but on energy. That's what will get you up in the morning, ready to take on the world.

You've Got to Market It

Once you've found your passion, let's talk just a bit about marketing that passion.

In Michael Gerber's book, *The E-myth,* he talks about the different kinds of people that are inside each one of us: the technician, the manager, and the entrepreneur. Let's say someone has a job as a mechanic, and he can fix cars like nobody else. The mechanic thinks to himself, "I could start a business, an auto mechanic shop, and make a bunch of money." Yet if he has no idea how to sell, offer, or market that service, no customers will show up. He might be the best auto mechanic in the world, but if no one comes to his business, he's going to fail.

Business owners are not in the businesses they think they're in. They're actually in the marketing of that business.

In other words, an auto mechanic isn't in the business of repairing cars, he's in the business of marketing his auto repair shop. A crucial point that most business owners miss is this:

If you can't sell your goods or services, if you can't get people into your business, you're going to fail.

Understanding the marketing of your business and your passion is paramount to being successful. You have to look at it as a flowing pipeline, and constantly be doing something to fill your pipeline by getting new people in the door. A typical mistake I see owners make is that they'll get a flood of customers and then stop marketing. When those customers dry out, there's nobody in the pipeline to replace them. As a business owner, you have to be constantly on the lookout for ways to get new customers, even while you're servicing the customers you already have.

I know of one restaurant that's still in business, and the only reason is because the owner goes to networking meetings and is *constantly* out in the community. If she didn't do that, she'd have closed her doors a year ago. She's out there talking to people, inviting them to her restaurant. She does catering; she offers free samples. The only reason they're still in business is because she's been willing to do that. Many businesses fall into the trap of "If I build it, they will come." That's dangerous thinking.

You can't just build a better mouse trap and expect people to buy that mouse trap if they don't even know it exists.

Getting the word out is the single most important function of any business, hands down.

What I really want you to know is that you have to be willing to become a master marketer of your business. You have to be disciplined enough to learn that skill set for yourself, because nobody will understand your business like you do. Nobody will understand your customers like you do. Nobody will understand the value and benefits of your products and services like you do. So you have to be the driving force behind the marketing of your passion, or it's not going to work.

The Platinum Rule

You remember the Golden Rule, don't you? The Golden Rule says, "Do unto others as you would have them do unto you."

Just one problem: I'm not you, and you're not me. The idea of "I'm going to do to you like I want you to do to me" is all about me.

The Platinum Rule is different.
It says, "Do to others what they would have you do to them."

How you would like to be treated may be very different from how I would like to be treated. The Platinum Rule respects those differences.

The Golden Rule is grounded in sound philosophy and it's just plain decent to be nice and kind to people. But, if you want to make a greater impact and have a valuable business, you won't be focusing on doing unto others as they do unto you. You will focus on doing to others as they would have you do to them. That's going to trickle down throughout your entire business, from the way you handle customer service, to the way you deal with complaints, to the way you treat your employees, to the way you service your clients and vendors.

Breaking Out of the Bubble

We all tend to live in these little bubbles of self-awareness and our own needs and wants. The Platinum Rule shatters those bubbles by saying, "It's not just about you; it's about everybody around you. It's about your actions because they impact everyone else." By being more self-aware, you're saying it's not simply about you. You're going to live a much happier and fulfilled life, because that Rule is going to loop back to your purpose of serving others, not yourself, first.

I think the Platinum Rule connects back to curiosity, too. It's about being genuinely interested, but this time in other people. Try to nurture that, try to figure out what people like, and like to do. This isn't just good for them; it's good for you too. When you show a genuine interest in others they find you more likeable, more relatable, and more empathetic; all good traits to have.

I had a conversation with my son Beau not long ago, when he had a buddy over and they were trying to figure out what to do. Beau wanted to play video games, but his friend wanted to throw the football around outside. I said,

"Beau, you need to do whatever your friend wants to do. He wants to go outside and throw the football." Beau said, "Well, the Golden Rule says to do unto others as I would have them do unto me, and I want to play video games, so I'm trying to get him to play video games because that's what I want done unto me." If Beau had taken the time to explore what was interesting to his friend, they may have had a better relationship at that point in time.

It all starts with self-awareness. We might not be self-aware because of the way we've always done things, and because that's the way we've always seen things done.

We might not even know another way of thinking exists, and that's the worst spot to be in, when you "don't know what you don't know." People need to realize there are other and better ways of doing things.

The Platinum Rule is all about the better way.

Give Value For Value

Traditionally, businesses have been running on the idea that they should sell their goods and services for the most amount of money, at the lowest-cost or quality possible.

The principle of value for value changes all that. For a business to be successful, it can no longer just give the least amount of products or services for the most amount of money. Value for value is about fair trade between two interested parties, and the basic philosophy is that I as a business owner am going to give you as much or more than what I get from you in return. If you want a highly successful business, you should begin asking,

"How much value can I give to get X amount of value in return? And if I can do that, is there any way to give a little more value and still have X be fair to me and my business? And then, can I give a little more value?"

Value For Value in Action

Have you ever seen *Toy Story*, *Cars*, or *Monsters, Inc.*? Those animated movies were created by a company called Pixar, and they are great at living the principle of value for value. When you see a Pixar film, there's no question that you got value for the eight to ten bucks you paid for a movie ticket. You're completely blown away by how exciting those Pixar movies are, and from the emotions they evoke. You leave a Pixar movie with an incredible feeling, like your socks have just been knocked off. You've just witnessed something majestic. That's value for value. Delivering a high-quality product or service for what customers deem a fair price. Pixar is obviously delivering; they're making tons of money.

When you buy a product and say to yourself, "I would have paid $20 for that instead of just $10," you know that company is delivering value. It's fair to them, it's fair to you, and the consumer feels like what they got far outweighed what they had to give up to get it. That's how you live value for value.

Exceed Expectations

In today's economy, many people are content with simply meeting expectations, but

Over the long term, the value of your business will be determined by your willingness to not simply meet expectations, but exceed them on every front possible.

Whether it's products, services, how you handle issues, or how your staff treats customers, all of those things can be lived by the principle of value for value.

Let's look at the example of how people are being treated when they walk into your office. Do they feel like they're welcomed? Is it a warm, friendly environment for them? The value they're giving at that moment is their time and their attention. It's called "paying attention" because they are paying you with their attention for something in return. They're paying you with their time, and that's a valuable thing they're giving you. You have to respect that, so go over and above treating them in ways that not only meet their expectations, but exceed them.

There are a lot of other ways, in the spectrum of a business, to give value for value. Not just, "Here's my product or service, and that's your money, so let's make an exchange." There's got to be something more to it than that.

Giving value for value also ties into the Platinum Rule because it's understanding what others consider valuable, not what you consider valuable, and then either meeting or exceeding that expectation.

Think about how you feel when a parent, teacher, friend, or mentor really listens to you, really tries to understand where you're coming from and what you're going through – not because they're trying to get something from you, but because they're looking for ways to serve you. The notion of value for value falls in line with that.

More than Fair

Remember when you were little and you were always told to share, to play nice, and to be fair? Well, giving value for value means taking those concepts to the next level.

Your goal as a businessperson is not just to have a fair exchange, but to exceed that: to be more fair, to give more than you're expecting from people in return.

That turns the idea of just "playing fair" upside down, since playing fair is kind of like meeting the minimum expectation. Looking through the lens of value for value, keep asking the question, "How much more can I give this person than what they're giving me?"

Your referrals will go up, word-of-mouth will be off the charts, and people are going to want to do business with you because they know they'll get true value for value, and they know they won't feel like they've been taken advantage of. Do that on a consistent basis over time, and business will be so much easier for you. You'll start attracting people who want to do business with you because they've heard of the way you treat customers, they've heard of your integrity, they've heard about how generous you are. Some might think doing business that way means you're giving up a lot, getting the short end of the deal, but to me, it's the exact opposite.

As an example, my company was building a website for a client who came back with a lot of different requests. Although those requests were outside the scope of what we'd contracted with them to do, I sat down with my team and said, "We're going to do these things anyway," and we did them. We've gotten three more referrals from that same client, because we went over and above. Those with short-term vision might have said we would lose money on that deal, and that we should have cut it off. What if we had? If we were only looking at the job that way, we might have pulled the plug, but because I was looking at the bigger picture, it helped us in the long run. Yes, we didn't make as much money as we should have on that particular website job, but we more than made up for it with the referrals that same client sent our way because we treated him in a manner that was more than just fair.

Be a Servant Leader

A true shepherd is never behind his
flock; he's right out in front, leading.
Without any cajoling or convincing,
without any pushing or force, he
just walks, and they follow.

Do you know the difference between a sheepherder and a shepherd? A sheepherder stands behind the sheep, and has to herd them in a certain way because the sheep don't exactly respect the authority of the sheepherder. With the sheepherder, the animals have to be cajoled and driven. Sometimes the sheepherder has to use force, or get his sheep dogs to help. But shepherds...shepherds are different.

It's because they see him as a source of value – as someone who takes care of them, feeds them, grooms them, attends to them when they're sick or hurt. And they respect him.

Servant leaders are the same way. If you want your people to follow you, you must be ready to serve them. Let's talk about some ways you can do that.

Share Your Vision

One way to be a servant leader is to always share your vision. Be transparent about what you're doing and where your business is going.

A lot of the time, we try to keep that information close to our vest, while telling our employees their job descriptions without any explanation of the big picture. When that happens, those employees feel like just another cog in the wheel, like they don't benefit the company they work for beyond that. Those employees don't understand what the company's entire vision is all about, and they don't understand what that company is trying to produce.

Tell your employees, "You're not just an individual here; you're part of something greater, part of this team, this family." We might not necessarily think of that as serving people, but what it does serve is their ego, their personality, and their way of being. Telling them this shows them that they're cared for, not just viewed as human resources (which is a business-world phrase I despise because it's so impersonal). You don't ever want your employees to feel like they're just an asset to be taken advantage of in your business. Your main job as a leader is to help your employees become the very best versions of themselves that they can be.

Be Someone Who Will Do Whatever it Takes

Being a servant leader means being someone who's willing to show employees that you're prepared to do whatever is needed to get things done.

A lot of the time business owners might kind of sit in their office and not go down into the trenches. They don't understand their employees' positions, challenges, or even the opportunities they're facing on a daily basis because they're not willing to get their hands dirty. I'm not saying a business owner needs to go mop the floors, but he should show that he's *willing to*, sending the message of "we're all in this together." If I'm expecting employees to stay late to work on a project in order to get it done for a client, and I'm taking off at four o' clock, that's sending them the wrong message. They're being told that, to me, the project is not that important. I do believe in a division of labor, and don't believe a president or CEO should be doing all sorts of different jobs; that's why we hire employees. I do think, though, that if a crisis time comes, that employer should be right there in the middle of it, out in front of his troops.

As leaders, we have to be the person who's out in front because that's what being a leader means – not someone who's standing behind the scenes, letting his team be the face of his business. A leader is out in front, guiding and leading his team to success.

The servant leadership model is that you seek first to serve your employees, clients, and vendors, and if you do, they will follow you without any force or coercion. That's servant leadership at its best.

Money & Debt

In business, cash is king. Not having enough cash just about sunk us in 2009 and 2010 because I'd invested every last penny into either the business, real estate, or some other non-liquid asset. I might have appeared to be very wealthy on paper, with a great net worth, but I had no cash.

When the economy tanked, I'd have been much better off sitting on a pile of cash versus having a bunch of real estate assets. We bought a building and houses and other assets. If that situation was going on now, it would have been okay, since the economy is turning around. Our business is back up, and we're doing well; cash flow is no longer a problem. But back then, it was a very challeng-ing, scary time period. Having assets that I couldn't tap into was frustrating. I couldn't even get a loan on them because my tax returns showed our net income as taking a hit, due to the recession. Even though I was getting a paycheck every two weeks, the business losses appeared on my tax return. I had all of that money sitting there, just out of my grasp. I would have saved myself a lot of headaches and pain if I'd only had some emergency cash on hand. Had things gone just a little differently, gotten gradually worse than they were, I wouldn't be sitting here talking to you. I'd be out looking for a job somewhere. It was that touch-and-go at the time. The point is you should always keep an emergency fund of cash for those unexpected situations that are bound to come up.

Managing your cash flow effectively is one of the most important skills you can learn in business! Hire the right professionals to help you, like accountants and financial advisors, and take the time to learn about profit-and-loss statements, balance sheets, and credit.

It All Adds Up

Debt can also be an unforgiving master. Be wary of the lure of a low monthly payment that's very small compared to the value of the asset. You might think to yourself, "I could afford that," but the more small monthly payments you have, the more it all adds up to something bigger. Should a dip in your business occur and you're overextended, you're going to get into trouble really fast. Businesses can be like a house of cards. Many "stable" businesses you might see across the nation are only a month or two away from having the whole thing crumble. A lot of businesspeople might think they're doing great, but if they miss a payment or if a big client doesn't pay for two months in a row, that business will be wiped out. In our business, we've tried to lessen that risk by building up cash reserves and opening lines of credit, but it's just dangerous to run anything at high levels of debt. An unexpected dip can set you back, big time.

The reason debt is so dangerous is because it provides instant gratification. It might be cool to be able to buy that new car, or go on that vacation on the credit card, but if you don't have money on hand and put even more credit on the card during that vacation, look out. Like I said, any little dip. Sure, it might be nice to have that new piece of equipment for your business, the one that's going to make things run more swiftly and efficiently. You just have to make sure that the payment amount you're on the hook for isn't going to be taking too big of a bite. You might try to plan as well as possible for your business, but there's always going to be that certain something you didn't plan for, that thing you couldn't see coming, and that could knock the whole thing down.

Debt is a Tool

The point is not that debt is bad. Borrowing money you need to grow your business can be a great strategy, but there needs to be an understanding of what's too much. We need not be so risk-shy that we don't use any debt at all, because that will stunt growth, but I think there's a right way to play it. Debt is a tool to be used, one you have to be strategic with, one you have to think through. There are many cases where debt can be okay, like when you're trying to expand or bring on new employees that can help you get to the next level. In that case, it's an investment that can be used very well. But, if you're just trying to keep up with the Joneses, buying luxury items to make yourself look better and improve your social status or spending money that creates no value for your company, that's a horrible way to use debt, and you should avoid it.

Look at all debt with a keen eye because businesses that take on debt casually can have it become a monster that comes back to bite them, one that eats away at everything else.

A Final Point to Consider About Money

As your business begins to grow, you will have people you have to pay on a regular basis: employees, vendors, and the government (in the form of taxes) to name just a few. But don't forget to pay yourself! One of the main reasons for starting a business is to provide you and your family with a lifestyle that you want.

Pay it Forward

Over the course of your life you will meet people who will need your help. As a successful business owner, you're going to be in a perfect position to offer that help. Remember, no business owner makes it alone. This isn't something you can do by yourself. A lot of people get drawn to the idea that being an entrepreneur means they can work by themselves and that they won't have to depend on anybody else. That's dangerously misleading. All of us have to depend on others, and all of us will need mentors who help us.

When you get to a certain level, and even before you get to that level, you should constantly be looking for ways to extend a hand out to somebody else. You need to pay it forward and help others out. That's what makes the world go round.

It Comes Back

I was talking to a group of salespeople not long ago during a training session. We were talking about the Pay it Forward principle and one of them asked, "Well, what if you do something really nice or valuable for someone, but they never pay you back?"

I said, "You can't look at it through that microscopic lens. You've got to look at it on a macro level.

As long as you're always paying it Forward, it's going to come back.

It may not come back to you directly from the person you've helped, but it will come back to you through other people who will help you." In other words, you've got to look at the net change, 'what I put in versus what I get back over time.' If you're doing it just for the sake of getting something back, you're doing it wrong.

That's not the reason for this principle of paying it forward. The reason for paying it forward is not just to become a better business owner, spouse, parent, or friend. It's to become a better person, a better human being.

This goes back to living that higher purpose we talked about earlier.

The reason you're doing all of this is because you were put on this earth with the responsibility to make it a little bit better than when you got here.

If you put this principle into practice, when you leave this earth, you will have made it better than it was when you arrived. That's what paying it forward is about.

In the early 1930s, a man named Napoleon Hill wrote a book called *Think and Grow Rich* that went on to sell millions of copies. In it, he described "17 Success Principles" that people used to become wealthy. One of those was "Going the Extra Mile." He always talked about doing more than what was asked of you. Paying it forward is about being in a position to help other people get to where they want to be, without any expectations.

Whatever you want to call it—karma, good will, whatever—we need to embrace the idea that doing good is not about making us feel better or about getting back good karma. As human beings, doing good isn't just optional, it's a necessity. It's ingrained in our DNA, but we suppress it sometimes, and we shouldn't. It is our responsibility as individuals and as human beings to encourage paying it forward as much as possible.

How to Pay it Forward

You should constantly be on the lookout for ways to pay it forward. Some of these ways might include:

- Being a mentor (someone who gives advice) to those around you
- Supporting small businesses financially by purchasing their goods and services or by sending them referrals
- Freely sharing your knowledge and expertise
- Introducing people you know to other people you know who may benefit from such an introduction (For example, once I introduced a lady I knew who was looking for a job to a friend of mine who was hiring. They hit it off and he hired her shortly after.)

I cannot stress the importance of the principle of paying it forward enough. It always comes back around, sometimes when you least expect it.

To illustrate this, let me tell you a story about when this happened in my own life. Recently an acquaintance of mine approached me about starting a new business and needed to have a website built and business cards made. Normally it is our policy to charge for those items *before* starting work on them, but I knew this person wasn't in a position financially to do that. So I set up a payment plan for her and billed her for the work over a six-month period, even though we built the site and printed her business cards right away.

Since doing that for this client, she has sent me over $10,000 in work from people she has referred to us – all because I took the time to understand her situation and give a little something of myself first.

Building the Business YOU Want and Living a Balanced Life

There's no blueprint for running a business. If there was, every business would be exactly the same, and there would be no reason to have multiple companies within the same industry, because they'd all be identical.

Building the business you want means creating something that's compatible with the person you are. It's about what's going to keep you excited and passionate over a long period of time.

If you don't build a business you love, one that really speaks to you and who you are, you're not going to have a very easy time in five, ten, fifteen, or twenty years because that business is not going to feel authentic.

Someone hearing that you're going to start your own business might predict you'll have a headache with your employees and with all of the typical business issues. That doesn't have to be the case. You might not choose to have a lot of employees. You can work alone; you can work with one or two different people. Nothing says you have to work with a large staff. On the other hand, you might decide that you want to build a huge company with thousands of employees because you want to create jobs and go big. That's fine, too.

It all begins when you figure out where you want to go. So many times people equate success with a lot of money, but that's not necessarily true. Success is however you define it. If it means having a thousand employees on a billion dollar payroll, that's what you should shoot for. If it means making enough money to spend three days a week at your cabin in the mountains, that's the type of business you should build. Remember, there's no right or wrong answer here. Your own definition of success is what fuels everything.

There's No Right or Wrong Way

This is more about discovering who you are – what's going to make you feel the most comfortable, the most alive. That's the sort of business you need to build.

Being told you have to do things in a certain way is an old-fashioned idea.

Here's an example: I know of a woman who runs a pizza company. She decided one day that she would sell monthly memberships to her pizza parlor. For $50 a month you could get $75 worth of pizza during that month. She was told nobody would buy a membership, and that people would never pre-pay for pizza like that. Fortunately, she didn't listen and went ahead and sold memberships anyway. She's now built a huge, thriving business based on an idea that people told her she couldn't do. Building the business you want means having an understanding of who you are, what's important to you, and what sort of lifestyle you want. Then you can create a business model that supports your vision.

So many people are doing things they don't like for a living. I think the reason is that they tend to bend to the pressure of building a certain type of business, based on what they think people expect of them. When you live out other people's expectations, you can't live out your own expectations. Not living your own vision and not living your own life is what creates that feeling of emptiness, the feeling that something is missing, that you're not living the life you were meant to live.

Building the business YOU want is not about catering to the expectations of other people, society, or your industry. It's about how you want to run your business and about the way you want

*to develop your products or services.
It's about figuring out what kind of
customers you want, what sort of
employees you want to hire, and who
you want to do business with, both
short term and for the long haul.*

That's much more important than conforming to what society expects.

Finding Your Own Brand of Balance

For me, the line between my personal and business life is very fuzzy. There's not really a line. For some people there's a very clear break. They have "work time" and they have "personal/family time." For me, my life is my work and my work is my life. That may be how you want to live too.

Or, maybe you build a business that lets you work a few hours a day and the rest of your time is spent surfing or reading or going places with your family. The point is that you just need to find what feels natural to you. You hear of these people living a "balanced life," who feel like it's bad if they're working too much. To me, it's about building the lifestyle you want. If that lifestyle means you're at work for twelve hours a day, but you're bringing your kids with you to work sometimes or you're incorporating some fun activities, then you're living a balanced life.

The term "balance" means different things to different people anyway, like beauty being in the eye of the beholder. Balance is a personal decision, so you'll have to figure out what that means to you and how you're going to live that balance. You can't ignore it, thinking it's not important and not something you need to focus on. You need to look at it, and look at it very carefully.

I think the happiest entrepreneurs are those whose lines between work and play are blurry; it's all kind of one. To them, there's no such thing as a business or personal life; it's just life.

The more they can live that kind of life, the better it is. Back before the industrial revolution, that's how life was. If a person was a farmer, they woke up and tended the fields or the livestock. They did the work that needed to be done on the farm, and they didn't go home after work – their whole life *was* work, and their whole life was play. It was all balanced perfectly because that was the lifestyle they'd chosen.

You Know What's Right For You

The main point is to be careful around critics who want to look at your life and call it unbalanced. They don't know you, they don't understand you, they don't know how you live, they don't know what's important to you, and they don't necessarily share your value system. The biggest piece of advice that I want you to know about principle is this: Do what feels natural and authentic. If you're happy and you're plugging along, and everything's going great in your life working twenty hour days because that's who you are, that's okay. If you only want to work five hours a week because that's who you are, then that's okay, too (as long as you're meeting your financial and emotional needs and can build a business that affords you that lifestyle). I personally think it would be kind of hard to work only five hours a week, but if you can do it, more power to you, and that's the point.

We spend so much of our lives doing what we think is expected of us, and not nearly as much time doing what WE expect of us. I think we should live up to our own highest expectations. Nobody should have a higher expectation of you than you. That's not to be left up to society, parents, teachers, or whomever. You need to hold myself to a higher standard, knowing that when it comes to building a business, what you identify with will become a part of your identity.

This is really about always striving to be the very best version of you that you can be.

What's right for everyone else in the world is irrelevant. It makes me laugh and always confuses me when I go to a restaurant and someone asks their waiter, "Which do you like better, this entrée or that one?" Why would someone ask another person a question like that? Are the waiter's taste buds exactly the same as theirs? Likewise, why would we ask someone else if they liked one movie better than another? *They're not you.* You need to make your own determination. Go see both movies, and figure it out.

You just can't build a world-class business without becoming a world-class person.

If you're going to be an entrepreneur, you're going to have to learn to be decisive and responsible for your actions. Build your business with an attitude of, "This is the kind of life I want to live, this is how I'm going to live, and I'm making no apologies for it." Be okay with that. I think in a lot of ways, that's a big key to your happiness.

Diversify Your Wealth

We live in a culture that believes in spending money just as fast as we make it. I want to help you to avoid that trap. I want to show you that there are other options for your money. You don't have to go and spend all of it; you can invest it and make it work for you.

There's that old saying, "Don't put all your eggs into one basket." That means not putting all of your money in just one place. That's the idea behind this principle. Diversifying your wealth means buying different appreciating assets and other investments that will grow in value over time. This is different from just spending your money on things that don't hold their value over time. For example, once you start making a decent income, you will be tempted to buy things that decrease in value as time goes on. A boat that you buy for $20,000 may only be worth $10,000 a few years later. A rental home, on the other hand, will most likely increase in value, making you wealthier over time. The trick is to buy several different types of investments so that you aren't exposed to loss in any one area.

I used to reinvest all of my money back into my business until I realized that if I kept doing that, and if my business went away at some point, I'd be in a really bad spot. If I banked on my business being around forever, then I could be broke at some point because I could go out of business. The main purpose of my starting my business had been to extract money from it, but I needed something to do with that money because I didn't want to just spend it.

There are lots of other things I could have done with my money that would have been smarter than spending it. I wish I had purchased real estate at a younger age, when I had money. I wish I had purchased life insurance. I wish I had bought disability insurance, just in case I was hurt or incapacitated and couldn't work. Fortunately, that hasn't happened, but I know people it's happened to, and if they could go back, they would have paid for that extra expense.

Multiple Baskets

Diversifying your wealth means looking at four or five different things, different baskets you create to put your eggs into. I think that's important, and I wish I would have done it differently when I first started my company. If I had, I'd be way further ahead, and I'd have so much more wealth.

I wish I had invested in an IRA (a type of investment account) or retirement plan of some sort sooner. I wish I had purchased some stocks and bonds, and had just done some basic financial planning. I wish I hadn't purchased assets that lose value like a boat, fancy cars, and those types of things.

I wish I had used some of that money to build up a savings account. That would have saved me a lot of headaches when the economy tanked, back when I was left sitting there looking at a business and some real estate as my only two assets. Neither of those things had been liquid; I couldn't get money out of either one of them. I wish that I had built up a cash reserve at that time. I wish I had some stocks and some bonds and had just done some basic financial planning. I didn't do any of that because I thought the money was going to keep pouring in forever. That was a bad mistake, and it nearly unseated me.

If you are wondering about some of the ways that you can invest, here is a short list of examples:

- Real estate (houses, apartment buildings, commercial buildings)
- Stocks, bonds, or other types of investments
- Insurance protection
- Cash savings
- Invest back into your business

In the case of real estate, stocks, bonds, and investing back into your business, you are putting your money to work for you. As those investments increase over time, so does your personal wealth. Just as importantly, you need insurance and cash on hand to protect you when bad things happen (like if you become disabled or have a downturn in your business). Each of these investments plays a role in your financial life, and understanding them and putting them to work for you is crucial to your long-term financial health.

It Goes By Fast

Right now you probably don't think so, but time goes by very quickly. I remember groaning on the first day of high school because I had four more long years of school left. It flew by.

Especially now, I look back on the past ten years, and it seems incredible how fast it's all gone by. Then there will be the next ten years. The problem is that the older you get, the faster time goes by. That happens every year, with time going by faster and faster, and before you know it you've spent ten years of your life saying, "Oh, I'll invest in that later on," or, "I'll buy that real estate later."

Later comes way sooner than you think, and then it passes you by before you know it. You have to start planning for later early. Don't wait to begin investing your money. Start now.

The Magic of Compound Interest

When you put money in the bank, you earn interest. In other words, the bank will pay you a certain percent to use your money to make loans to other people. They make money by charging the borrower more than they are paying you. For example, you may deposit $100 into a bank savings account that pays you 5% interest. That means if you leave your money in the bank for a year, then at the end of the year you would have $105 in your account.

Compound interest makes this earning potential even more powerful, because after that first year you are now earning interest on your interest. Sounds confusing, right? Well here's how it works: after the first year you have $105 in your account. The bank will now pay you 5% on the $105, which will give you $110.25. If you had just earned 5% on the original $100 at the end of two years, you'd have $110. I know $.25 is nothing to get too excited about, but look what happens after several years of letting your money grow:

Year	Compound Interest	Simple Interest
1	$105.00	$105.00
2	$110.25	$110.00
3	$115.77	$115.00
4	$121.55	$120.00
5	$127.63	$125.00
6	$134.00	$130.00
7	$140.71	$135.00
8	$147.75	$140.00
9	$155.13	$145.00
10	$162.89	$150.00

Year	Compound Interest	Simple Interest
11	$171.03	$155.00
12	$179.59	$160.00
13	$188.56	$165.00
14	$197.99	$170.00
15	$207.89	$175.00
16	$218.29	$180.00
17	$229.20	$185.00
18	$240.66	$190.00
19	$252.70	$195.00
20	$265.33	$200.00
21	$278.60	$205.00
22	$292.53	$210.00
23	$307.15	$215.00
24	$322.51	$220.00
25	$338.63	$225.00
26	$355.57	$230.00
27	$373.35	$235.00
28	$392.01	$240.00
29	$411.61	$245.00
30	$432.19	$250.00
Total:	**$432.19**	**$250.00**

Look at the difference! By letting your money grow at just 5% per year at a compounded rate, you earn over $182 more than if you had just earned the 5% on $100 each year. That's the magic of compound interest, and why it is so important that you begin saving your money and investing it as soon as possible.

 # Talent is Overrated

Back when I was younger and wondering about a career, it finally occurred to me:

My success had more to do with my willingness to do things other people wouldn't or couldn't do. That was what would set me apart. Your success can be the same.

The idea that you have to be incredibly talented or really smart is overrated. Just about anyone who is mediocre in the talent area but who has a good work ethic will trump someone with natural talent and smarts any day of the week. We talk about genius like it's a rare thing that is hard to capture, but in reality, genius is simply the ability to solve problems in different ways and to work hard to continue solving those problems.

Have you ever watched the television show Duck Dynasty? It's about a family that started a business several years ago selling duck calls. The head of the family is a man named

Phil Robertson. When Phil started the company (called Duck Commander) back in the 1970s, he had no money, no resources, and no way of selling his handmade duck calls.

That didn't stop Phil. He just started going to every store he could think of to sell his duck calls, just a few at a time. Time after time he was told no. He never gave up. One day he went into a Wal-Mart and asked to see the manager. He told the manager that he was there to sell him duck calls. For whatever reason, this manager agreed to buy six duck calls. That small victory was all Phil needed.

From then on he was able to sell more and more of his duck calls, but that first year was pretty tough. He only sold about $8,000 worth of duck calls. Duck Commander now does several millions of dollars in business each year, but the company would never be where it is today without the incredible work ethic of its founder, Phil.

Through sheer determination, persistence, and hard work, Phil turned a tiny little duck call company into a huge enterprise.

I don't think people understand the level of commitment that takes. It has a lot less to do with talent and smarts than it has to do with sheer determination. It's the attitude of, "I'm going to do this, and nobody's going to stop me." That mentality has been lost in our society because people feel things should come easily to them. We live in a culture that says we can take one little pill to make us lose weight. Easy. Fast. A lot of the blame falls on us for creating that, but it's also created this illusion that we don't have to work hard, that if we're just ridiculously smart and talented, we can go places. That's often not true. I know people who are much, much smarter than I am, who haven't reached the heights that I've reached financially, yet they're smarter; I'll freely admit that. The difference is that I, and others who've been successful, do things on a daily basis that those smart people are unwilling to do. That's what separates us.

Genius vs. Determination

Thomas Edison invented the light bulb, and we think he's a genius, but it took him something like ten thousand tries to do it. His genius came from his dogged, sheer, and stubborn persistence, from not giving up. Can you imagine what might have happened had he decided to give up on try number 9,998? I'd be sitting here writing this out by candlelight.

Edison's example should give hope to anyone who says, "I'm not smart enough" or "I'm not talented enough to run a company or come up with great ideas." His story serves as proof that you can look at your life and say,

"*You know what? I can do this. Others who were not the smartest or most talented people in the room did it. Just by sheer hard work, I can do this.*"

Something that frustrates me about being an entrepreneur is that sometimes people tend to only see my success; they don't see what goes on behind the scenes that got me that success. Whenever I hear anyone saying, "He/she was an overnight success," I think that's misleading and dangerous thinking. No one is an overnight success. A guy named Gary Vaynerchuk, an innovative entrepreneur and someone I follow closely, said, "Sure, I was an overnight success; it only took me ten years to get to that night."

There is no magic pill or easy button, no blueprint that's going to guide you step-by-step through life. A lot of it is just going to come from your figuring stuff out as you go along, and from not being afraid to fail. As long as you keep getting back up, trudging forward, and putting in the work, you'll be successful. You should know that it is okay not to have all the answers. Keep working, keep trying, and never give up.

Understanding Different Types of Education

A word about education – and I want to be a little careful here because I don't want you to think that getting a college degree is bad – I believe that, in many cases, formal education can be somewhat overrated. This seems especially true if you're planning to be an entrepreneur.

Yes, there are things you can learn in college. Many colleges have great small business programs. However, the old-school idea that you've got to go to college and get an MBA to become a successful entrepreneur is, in my opinion, absolutely False.

There is a lot of value in school, but when you compare the long-term cost versus value, you have to decide if it's really going to be worth it. A lot of people agonize over how they're going to get their Masters Degree or PhD; they fret over what their major will be. If you plan to be an entrepreneur or business owner, you can put much less emphasis on formal education.

Don't get me wrong, I think it's good to have a college degree, and I have one. My degree helped me learn to think strategically and critically, but I'm glad I didn't put tons of effort into figuring out if mine was the right degree or not. That would have hindered me more than helped. I just bit the bullet, picked a business major, and went with it. Lots of people get to college and change majors two to three times, and that sets them back. They might be in school for six years before figuring out which degree they want. A lot of them still wind up hating their choice, anyway. I think we'd be better served by not spending as much time in that regard.

With that being said, I do think it is crucial that you never, ever stop learning. Do you know why, when you finish high school or college, the graduation ceremony is called "commencement"? It's because your life has just begun. In fact, continuing to learn even after you're out of school is so important, that's what the next chapter covers to motivate you.

Never Stop Learning

A friend and I were talking the other day about a guy we know who opened a new line of his business. When I had asked this business owner how in the world he'd found the materials for the new line, he replied, "I don't know, I guess I got on the Internet." The friend and I were laughing over that, thinking how twenty years ago, a business owner would have had to do extensive, incredibly frustrating searches within the Yellow Pages or whatever, just to have made things happen and make things work. We take for granted that we can get on the Internet these days and learn anything we want. Whatever we want to figure out, it's on the Internet somewhere.

You live in such a unique era, literally holding in your pocket the most powerful computer the world has ever known, by way of your smart phone. We have access to all of the information we could possibly need, literally at our fingertips. I think we take that for granted. The fact is, learning about virtually anything in the world is easier than it's ever been.

Apart from the Internet, let's explore some different ways you can keep learning.

Make Use of Mentors

There are incredible, nontraditional opportunities to continue learning, and mentorship is one of them.

There's no reason to reinvent the wheel, especially when you're an entrepreneur. Somebody, somewhere, is doing what you want to do for a business.

Maybe not exactly the way you would do it, but they've laid some groundwork. There are people out there who are more than happy to share that information, if you just ask.

A person with experience that you can trust, someone who you know is going to help you out, is a valuable component to your success – especially since entrepreneurs can sometimes be the loneliest people on the planet. Entrepreneurs are sometimes surrounded by non-entrepreneurs and non-business owners, who don't understand the problems, challenges, and opportunities that accompany running a business. Mentorship is key – to have someone close to you whom you can bounce ideas off, run projects by or just get advice from is priceless.

Something to keep in mind: There is no person you can't learn from. If you're not constantly learning things from everyone around you, that's your fault, not theirs. Everyone has something to offer, some knowledge to give. Seek out opportunities to interact with people, whether it's a mentor, client, vendor, or a colleague. Continually be on the lookout for interactions. You might think what you're doing is just casual chit-chat, that you're going to get to know that person a little and then part ways. It's much more strategic to enter an interaction with the thought, "What can I learn from this person?"

Every person has something of value, some knowledge you can use. Keep your eyes and ears open for what that is. You won't know what it will be beforehand, or if what you learn will be useful down the road, but keep an open mind. It's a great way to approach relationships.

The Mastermind

Now we come to something that's near and dear to my heart: mastermind groups. Mastermind groups are small groups of people who meet on a regular basis to discuss ideas, talk about business challenges, and talk about any available opportunities. Mastermind groups are like having a board of advisors, almost like a group of friends having weekly or monthly discussions about how to solve various problems.

The concept here is to exchange ideas, because when you exchange ideas, you're creating something more powerful than if your idea stood alone. Think of it this way: if I have an apple and you have an apple, and you and I trade apples, you still have only one apple, and I still have only one apple. However, if we were to exchange ideas instead of apples, we would now both have two ideas. Your idea plus my idea could create a third, fourth, or fifth idea. The trading of ideas makes them exponentially expand, which is why Napoleon Hill called this method a mastermind. When you get two or more people together to talk about ideas, another mind – a "mastermind," is formed.

Mastermind groups are a great way to solve problems or attack challenges that might be impossible to solve on your own.

Break Out the Books

Next point: crack the books. Almost everything I know I learned through reading. I'm a big reader, and I think anyone who ever achieved any level of success was more than likely a very big reader. Sure, there are people out there who have never read a book in their lives and are successful, but I'd guess that they are very rare. More than likely, the successful people you'll meet in your lifetime are successful because they read a lot.

The beauty of reading is that you can take ideas you might have never considered before and put your own spin on them when applying them to your life.

You might only get one or two ideas from each book you read, but if you combine those ideas, they could create something powerful. The point is, it is up to *you* to find the value in everything that you read. If you don't see the value in the books you're reading, you're doing it wrong. Always be on the lookout for hidden knowledge that you can use.

Read, Listen, Learn

Reading goes beyond books. There are blogs I follow and podcasts I listen to, and in most cases they're free or very low cost to access. These resources are available and cover virtually anything you'd like to learn about. It's easy to be really proactive and consistent with learning, just by carving out time each day to read or listen. That will go a long way towards helping you continually learn over time. One of my favorite things to do is to listen to at least one TED talk daily (www.ted.com). These talks, which are about twenty minutes long, are a habit for me, and I often listen to talks that have nothing to do with the things I'd typically be interested in.

Along that same vein, once every two or three months, I visit a bookstore and buy four or five magazines that I have no interest in whatsoever. Not long ago I bought a knitting magazine, just because I thought it was important to see things through a different perspective as much as I could. That helps us communicate better, builds stronger relationships with people, and helps us to empathize and build empathy. There are so many benefits to be enjoyed from learning as much as we can.

The world is vast; there are so many things out there, with endless opportunities for us to learn. We can easily broaden our horizons. There's no reason to stay at the level we're at.

The other day I saw this little animated GIF (Graphics Interchange Format) that showed how a sewing machine works, how the needle went down through the material, grabbing another loop of string and pulling it back up, how it goes in a circle, over and over. I'd always wondered about that. Though the video only lasted six seconds and I might never use that information, you just never know. Maybe I'll get an idea inspired by that little GIF on how to present something, to use it as an analogy in a story I'm telling. Maybe when I'm talking about some sort of marketing technique I'll equate it to how a sewing machine needle goes down and picks up another strand, and how it's all happening behind the scenes. This could easily tie into some sort of an analogy, especially if I'm talking to someone who sells sewing machines for a living. You never know what's going to come in handy.

You'll Use It Eventually

It's good to have a broad range of interests because you're going to encounter a broad range of personalities. When I'm giving a presentation, the group I'm talking to often varies by profession. For example, if I'm presenting on social media management, what I say is going to be different depending on whether I'm talking to a group of retail store owners or financial advisors. If I don't take the time to understand that group and learn what their world is all about, I'm going to have a hard time communicating with them.

If you're good at empathizing, good at building relationships, and good at communicating, that's going to trickle down in a positive way throughout your whole business. You'll deal with employees, clients, and vendors much better.

Everything you learn and everything you do touches everything else you're going to do in a way that might not be clear from the outside looking in, but the things you experience are going to be important.

Our lives are all interconnected and we have experiences to share with one another that will enrich us and make our time here on Earth better in every way.

Now it's Your Turn

What do you want to be when you grow up?

That is a question you are going to hear a lot as you get older. I hope that after reading this book you will consider starting your own business one day. I truly believe that being an entrepreneur is one of the noblest things you can do for yourself and for society.

You don't have to be an entrepreneur of course. Maybe you want to be a doctor or a lawyer or a teacher. Those are noble pursuits as well. Either way, the things you learned in this book should help you become the very best entrepreneur, doctor, lawyer, or teacher that you can be.

Just keep in mind that the world needs more people who live by the principles outlined in this book. The world needs more people who practice the Platinum Rule. It needs more servant leaders. It needs more business owners and employees that live their lives by giving value for value. The world needs someone like you.

We need your ambition and your hard work and your imagination. We need you to help lead us and our economy into the future. The simple fact that you read this far tells me that you are not ordinary. You are extraordinary.

You are going to face many challenges and obstacles throughout your lifetime. But, you will also have incredible opportunities come your way as well. Remember, the only real difference between an obstacle and an opportunity is the way you choose to see it.

It is my hope that you will use the principles in this book to guide you in taking advantage of the opportunities that life has to offer. I hope that these principles will not just make you a better businessperson, but a better human being as well.

I wish you the best of luck on your unique journey!

Glossary

Advantage: favorable, gainful, positive things or situations that can lead to success

Asset: resource, property, holding, or item that is of value and can be readily sold to obtain money

Appreciating asset: asset having a value that grows over time, due to inflation, rates of interest, or fluctuating supply and demand

Authentic: true, real, natural

Capitalist: someone who puts their money into a business with the expectation of a positive outcome and profit

Cash reserve: easily accessible money that's set aside for 'just in case,' or money kept readily on hand should an individual or company require immediate funds

CEO: Chief Executive Officer

Client: person who uses your services or advice, someone getting help through your services

Colleague: an associate, someone working within the same career field or within the same office setting

Compatible: harmonious with who you are as a person, well-suited, able to exist with, connected to

Compound interest: money accumulated when interest is combined to the amount of a deposit or loan

Corporate: being a combined part of a corporation or group of people in action and thought

Customer: someone who buys goods or services from your company

Debt: money or its equivalent that's owed to someone else, an obligation

Diversify: to invest money in several different places, create variety

Economy: the way a community or country manages resources as a people, an organized way to determine productivity and prosperity

Employer: an individual or a business that hires one person or many people, and pays them for the work they do.

Enterprise: an undertaking or project, often done with a bold and adventurous attitude

Entrepreneur: someone who sets out to create an enterprise, using large amounts of ambition, gumption, and possibly taking on some risk

Franchise: the right to operate a certain pre-existing system or business with set guidelines previously built into it; rights given to certain individuals to use specific trademarks and methods

Goods: products of a satisfactory or quality nature

Impact: influence or the effects that occur when the mind meets with a new concept

Integrity: honesty, of good moral character, unimpaired

Investments: putting money into something like a business, buying shares of stock, or any other venture with the intention of gaining more money by doing so

Leverage: using money to decrease the responsibility for any financial loss

Line of credit: A source of money that an individual can tap into through a bank, the government, or various other means, usually secured by 'collateral', which is property promised to those lending the money if the loan is not paid back in full

Macro world: a world or worldview that's large, grand in its scope

Marketing: actions that advertise, in an effort to sell products or services

Mastermind group: first coined by Napoleon Hill, author of *Think and Grow Rich,* who defined the groups as a "coordination of knowledge and effort, in a spirit of harmony between two or more people, for the attainment of a definite purpose"

Mentor: a teacher who is considered trustworthy and to have wisdom; one who supports

Micro world: particularly small worldview, narrowed scope

Minutia: the smallest of precise, often unimportant details

Moral compass: guidelines that go into effect when a person is making any decision based on his or her beliefs

Net income: a person's or business's earnings for goods or services sold, minus the cost to provide them, the expenses, and the taxes that must be paid,; sometimes called the 'bottom line'

Networking: a gathering of people with the intention to support each other, share information, promote their services to each other, and work within a common interest

Option: the opportunity to make a choice, the selection of one choice over another

Passion: something that stirs the emotions or strong feelings

Pay it Forward: doing something for a person in order to pay back a good deed done for you by someone else, coupled with the belief that the beneficiary will then 'pay it forward' to another person

Pension: a certain amount of money beyond wages that is paid into an employee's account on a regular basis, often meant to be used at the time of retirement

Philosophy: opinions and views formed through experience and study

Pipeline: route or method of conveying goods, materials, money, clients, etc., as in 'keeping the pipeline full'

Proactive: getting ready for something (possibly an event) in such a way that one is prepared, to have control over an outcome or situation

Products: an item or person that's a result of a process of efforts, as in 'your company's product' or 'he is a product of his education'

Profits: the money left over after subtracting employee wages and the cost of making a product or provision of service, sometimes called 'revenue'

Purpose: desired reason for doing something, determined motive

Qualifier: validating the meaning, idea, or legitimacy of something

Reassess: to view one more time in a different light, re-evaluate

Referral: the recommendation of a person, product or service to a potential customer or client

Relationship: any forming of an ongoing friendship or business involvement that connects people in some way

Risk: any action involving the likelihood or potential for loss

Self-reliance: relying in a trust and confidence in your own capabilities

Services: an act that is helpful, coming to the aid of someone, supplying something that is needed

Skill range: extent or scope of limits of an individual, determined by natural talent and ability

Solution: answer to a problem, problem-solving

Transparent: being open to the truth of any given situation, easily detected or understood

Value: something of importance or worth, in money, time, materials, or effort invested

Value system: a collection of morals and standards that combine to determine an individual's thoughts and behaviors

Vendors: people or businesses that sell or convey goods or services

Viable: an idea or object that has the capacity to survive and grow

Vision: anticipation of something (often positive) that could happen in the future, a perception of something having potential

Wages: payment made for labor done by the job, or by time frames like hourly, daily, weekly

Word of mouth: one of the most valuable sources with which a business can gain customers or clients, when a satisfied customer tells a potential customer about excellent goods or services they've received and recommends a business

Work ethic: involves honest, hard work and persistence, a core, integral belief in giving as much or more value than what that person is being paid for, for the sheer joy of being known as reliable and standing out in excellence

Credits

There may only be one author's name on the cover of a book, but it really does take a team to write one. I am very appreciative to those who have helped me take this book from idea to finished product.

My Aloha Publishing team – Maryanna Young, Amy Larson, Hannah Cross, and Nichole MacDowell – were instrumental in helping me turn my rambling and incoherent thoughts into a readable manuscript.

I want to thank my employees and colleagues at V-Squared Creative for their unwavering support and hard work. I could never do any of this without you.

Finally, I am grateful to my own two kids, Beau and Scarlett, for the innate curiosity and enthusiasm they have about my business and life in general. They were the impetus for getting this project rolling. My wife Kirsten deserves more kudos than I can muster for being the best mom in the world to them.

About the Author

Tobe Brockner experienced the thrill of entrepreneurism early in life, when he started his first business trading baseball cards in the second grade. After graduating from college, Tobe launched his first company, and has built it into a successful marketing firm. Tobe believes that entrepreneurism is an important career option that should be offered to every child. In his business life, he strives to live the principles of "purpose first and profits second," and providing "value for value" to every client. Tobe lives just outside Boise, with his wife, Kirsten, and his two young budding entrepreneurs, Beau and Scarlett.